P.T.S.D.

P.T.S.D.

PUTTING THE STORY DOWN

SAUNDRA T. RUSSELL

P.T.S.D.
PUTTING THE STORY DOWN

iUniverse books may be ordered through booksellers or by contacting:

iUniverse
1663 Liberty Drive
Bloomington, IN 47403
www.iuniverse.com
1-800-Authors (1-800-288-4677)

ISBN: 978-1-5320-3177-9 (sc)
ISBN: 978-1-5320-3178-6 (e)

Library of Congress Control Number: 2017913381

Print information available on the last page.

iUniverse rev. date: 10/13/2017

PTSD...

CONQUERING YOUR BATTLE WITHIN THROUGH

YOUR KNOWLEDGE UNIVERSITY

IN THIS YOUR SELF HELP WORKBOOK

★ ★ ★ ★ ★ ★ ★ (OPPORTUNITY + PERSEVERANCE = SUCCESS) ★ ★ ★ ★ ★ ★ ★

"MY MOST MEMORABLE VETERAN"

(NOTE: This is a true scenario; therefore, it has numerous quotes.)

It was the middle of a late December night
The full moon shone; but there was nary a light
It was around 3AM, in the still of the night
I was making rounds to see that everything was alright

When out of the darkness and deepest quiet
I heard "Help me, someone help me!"
A frail voice broke, as if in a riot.
I realized it was Major _____ in bed 44B

I hastened down the long dark hall
It was a 40 bed medical unit on the south of the 12th floor
To reach this veteran ...Wow! He did stand tall
I got to his room, he was waiting at the door

"Help me, help me", he cried out again
"The enemy has come and captured my men"
This veteran with PTSD was having a flashback
He was concerned about Jim and John and Jack

He needed to and wanted to talk it out
His voice was full of terror, yet it did have clout
I listened to his story of the war he had fought
He had many questions, and answers he sought

I gathered a few of the vets, who were awake
Together we listened and laughed at our mistakes
Mistakes at realizing answers were not to be had
We resolved nothing and it was so sad

I assured Major _____ I'd put in a request
For him to have a morning consult with one of the best
The best Provider to help with his PTSD and more
This veteran said he would be OK, he was sure

He then asked if I would pray with him
Not for his welfare; but, for that of his friends
He said "On the battlefield they lived and died
But 'memories' were on their brains forever fried"

He said the prayers would heal them all
For him, it meant he could always stand tall
Stand tall to salute the red, white and blue
Stand tall for the freedom won for me and for you

REMEMBERING WORDS FROM A VETERAN

'WOW...You know your initials spell 'STaR'?
A Nurse and Angel...a STAR, you are!

You are an Angel, You are a Star
You are the best Nurse, I've had thus far...
You treat me kindly, You treat me good
You're the best Nurse in the neighborhood!!
You thank me for my years of service
I thank you for your service to my brothers and me...
I fought for our freedom, in the _____ war
Your spirit and service...I could not ask for more!

You've served me richly, healing me too
You've validated trauma I've been through...
You've listened to my stories, each night
You have helped me nightly through my fright!
I know your name, and I'll shout your name
'Cause whenever I called 'Nurse,, you came....
You are a Star, You are a Nurse
You are a STaR*healer...you're the first!!!'

GOOD NUTRITION EVERY MEAL

Make no mistake
Everyday you must take:

GOOD carbohydrates (whole grains), protein, fats/oils and fiber
Vitamin and mineral supplements, if needed
'B' and 'D' vitamin intake have been found to be important to health and healing
Include these in your intake everyday
Eating chicken, fish, fresh fruits, nuts,
Beans, seeds, eggs and enriched grains
Will provide these vitamins
EAT UP for good nutrition
Should be yours and to be in your meal plan every day!

Forget high cholesterol and trans fats and oils and limit intake of red meats
Include low fat milk, poultry, fish, legumes and nuts in the meal plan for the day
And make sure to use more of the monounsaturated and polyunsaturated fats
Say 'NO' to sugar, soda and salt; including sugary, and salty foods and snacks
Forget high cholesterol and trans fats and oils and limit intake of red meats
Include low fat milk, poultry, fish, legumes and nuts in the meal plan for the day
And make sure to use more of the monounsaturated and polyunsaturated fats
Read about it, write about it,
Make it a part of your life
Eat right, Eat well, Eat smart
With breakfast - you will start
You will start your day in a better way
Lunch and Dinner, to healthfully follow
Your nutrient rich meal plan for the day!

MY*KU PURPOSE

To help you, an AMERICAN HERO, to begin to recover from the traumatic events you were exposed to through STORYTELLING in a concise, brief and POETIC format that is easy, pleasant and hopefully enjoyable for you to do!

THANK YOU FOR YOUR SERVICE
STaR*KU

PTSD MY★KU DEDICATION

"My country 'tis of thee
Sweet land of Liberty"

Dear veterans everywhere
Gratitude to you, because you care...
Hope, Love and Peace are sent to you
For all that you have done and all you do
The same gratitude, hope, love and peace
Whether on the homeland or overseas
Goes to all who have served
Because these things are well deserved!

INTRODUCTION -PTSD

Is it now your time to be heard and conquer those traumatic memories?
Then, you may be interested in 'GETTING YOUR STORIES OUT'

Power in writing
Telling your stories
Sharing is healing
Divine enlightenment

Don't HATE...CONGRATULATE!

Congratulate yourself by doing something positive for yourself...

MY - It's yours, own it, it's all about you!

***KU - Keeping Up ***

***MY*KU = My keeping up*

Collection of MY*KU's = My Knowledge University

KNOWLEDGE is power
UNDERSTANDING empowers

'KNOWLEDGE UNIVERSITY'
It is the best way for me...
To express myself, you see

Sharing is healing at my Knowledge University

★★★**AFFIRMATION**★★★

My what, where, how, why and when
Comes 'FROM my BEAUTY WITHIN'...
For children, for women and for men!!!

★★★MANTRA★★★

Today I will live and be
Full of PEACE, LOVE, HOPE and JOY...
Toward MAN, WOMAN, GIRL and BOY
And each LIVING THING I see!!!

PTSD MY*KU INSTRUCTIONS

INSTRUCTIONS:

***Stop and give yourself time to reflect and think...

WHAT IS ON YOUR MIND?
WHAT IS BOTHERING YOU?
WHAT LIGHTS YOUR BELLY FIRE?

***Write down these thoughts...get that fire out...

ONE WORD OR A PARAGRAPH...WRITE IT DOWN!
Example: NIGHTMARES ARE MY MAJOR ISSUE...

***Organize these thoughts into key words...
Example: NIGHTMARES

***Write 3 sentences 7, 8, &/or 9 syllables each line…

Example: EVERY NIGHT I HAVE NIGHTMARES   (7)
THEY KEEP ME FROM GETTING MY REST...   (8)
THE NEXT DAY I CAN'T BE AT MY BEST!   (9)

* * * * * * * NOW YOU HAVE CREATED A MY*KU. * * * * * * *

MORE EXAMPLES...

To veterans who have served
Love, Joy, Peace, Hope: WELL DESERVED...
NOW IS YOUR TURN TO BE HEARD!!!

You have given us your best
You have been put to the test...
Now it is your turn to rest!

Peace and comfort you will find
No more being in that bind…
Just write down what's on your mind!

COMBAT

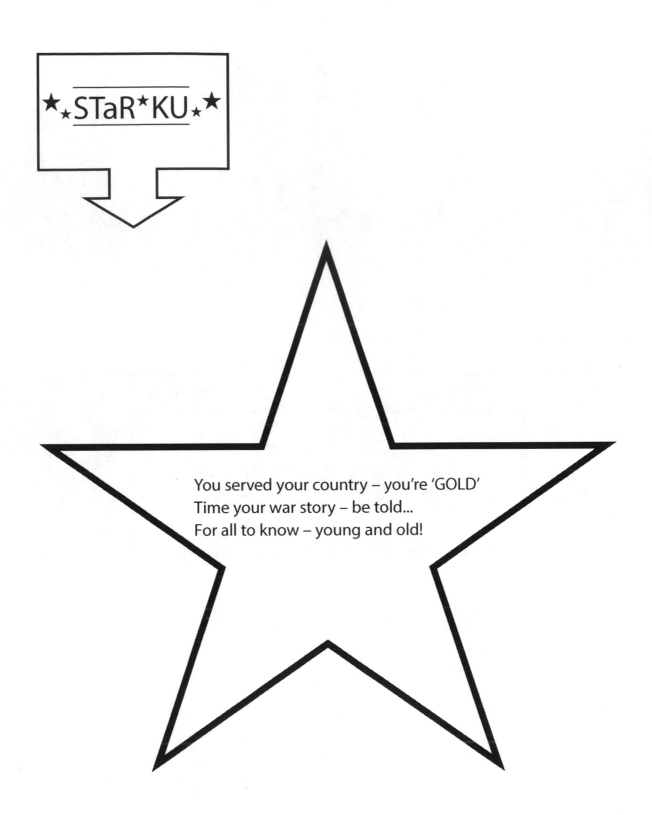

★.STaR★KU.★

You served your country – you're 'GOLD'
Time your war story – be told...
For all to know – young and old!

PEACE
THROUGH POETRY (My★KU)
STORYTELLING...
DONE!

COMFORT

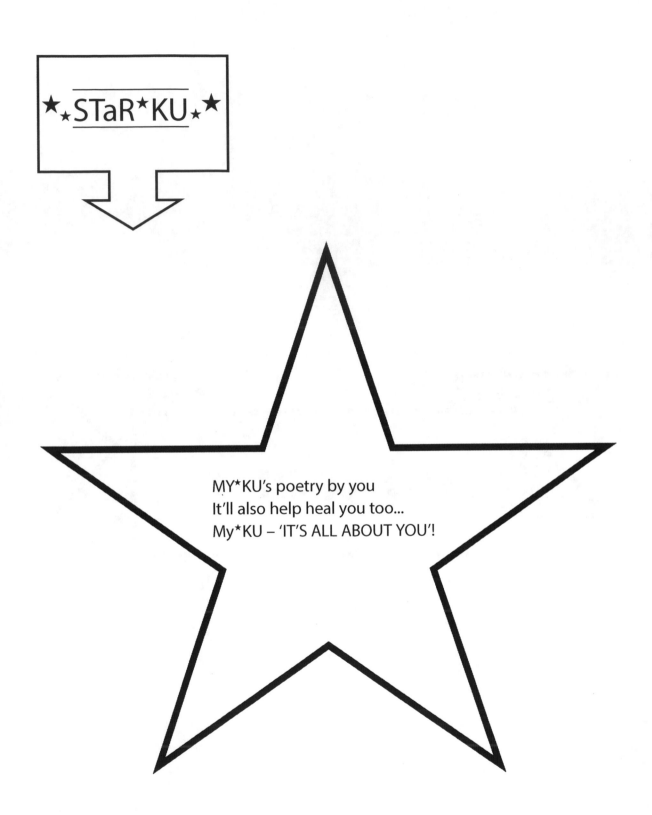

 STaR*KU

MY*KU's poetry by you
It'll also help heal you too...
My*KU – 'IT'S ALL ABOUT YOU'!

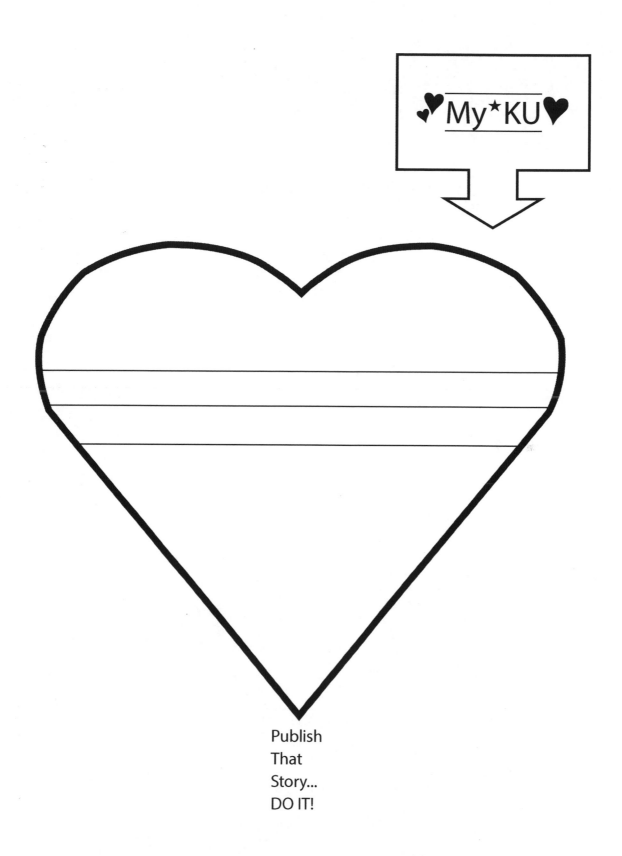

Publish
That
Story...
DO IT!

COURAGE

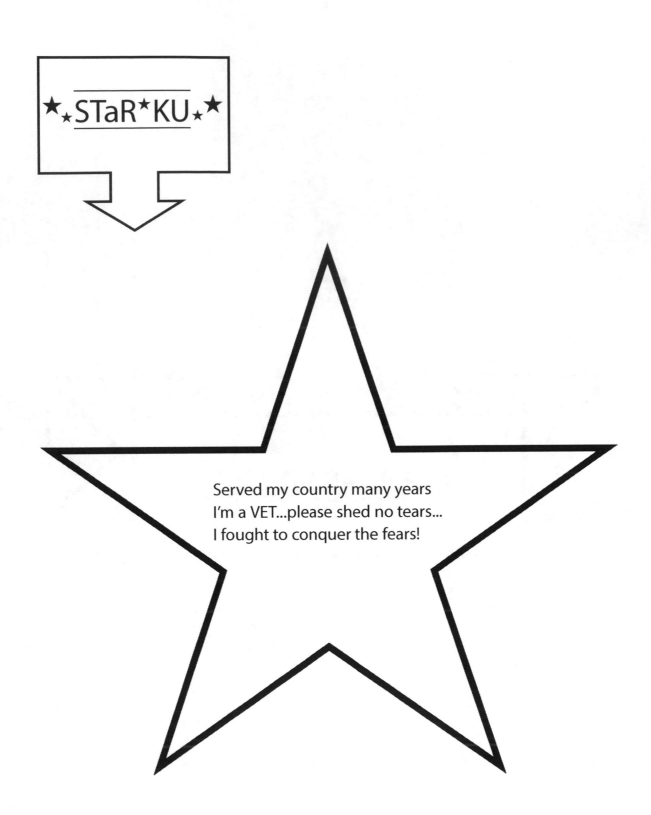

Served my country many years
I'm a VET...please shed no tears...
I fought to conquer the fears!

Poetry
That
Says you
Did it

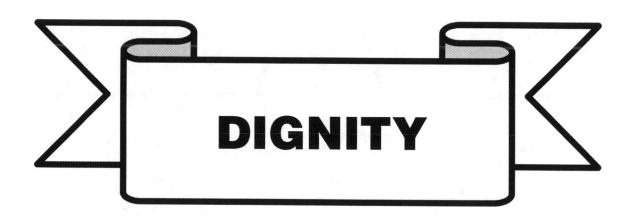

DIGNITY

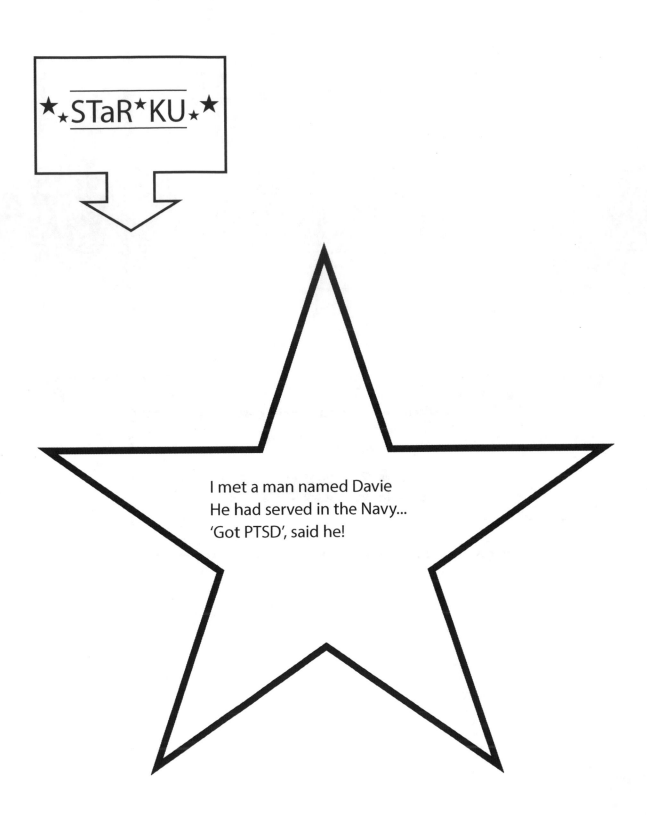

PAX...
TOLERANCE
SEMPER
DILIGO VESTRI

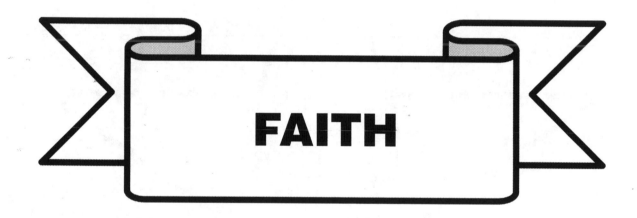

FAITH

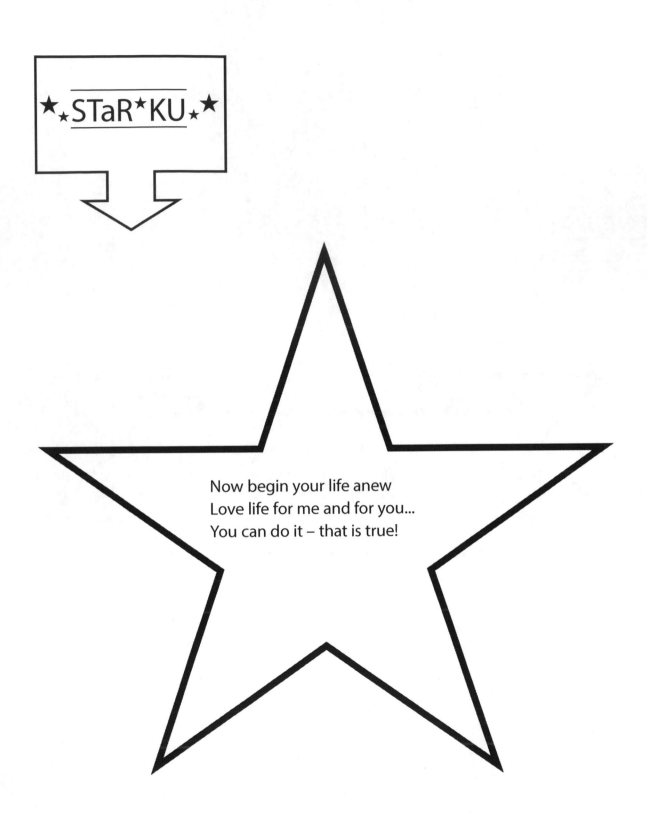

Now begin your life anew
Love life for me and for you...
You can do it – that is true!

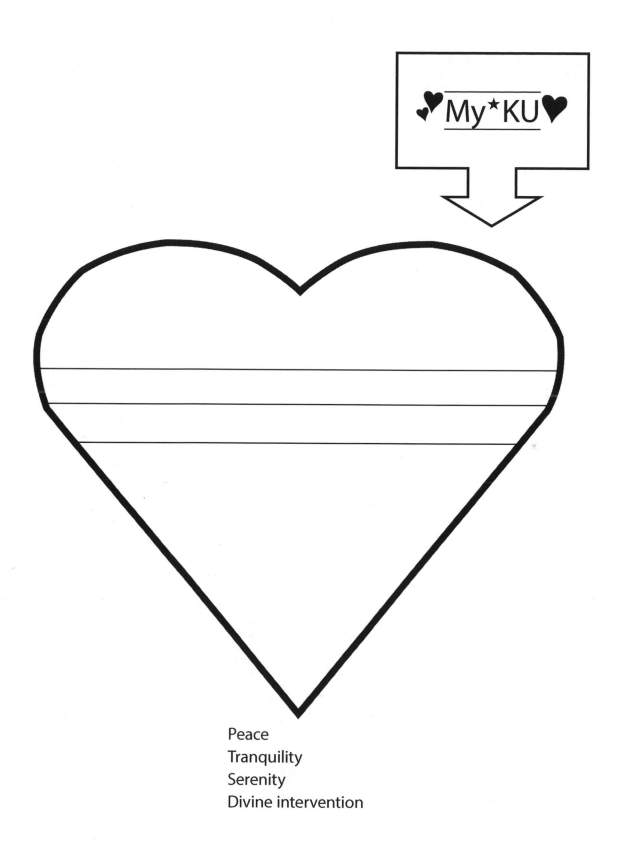

Peace
Tranquility
Serenity
Divine intervention

29

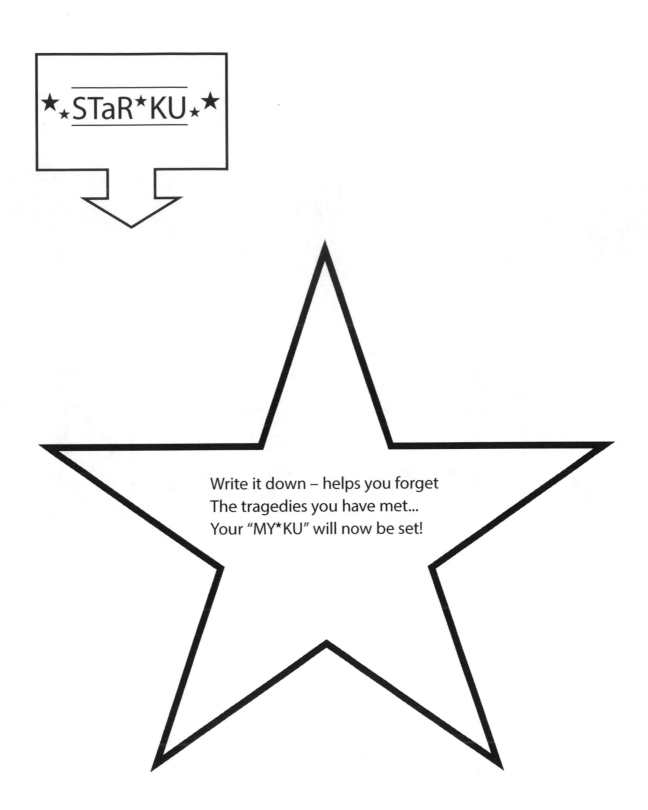

★.STaR★KU.★

Write it down – helps you forget
The tragedies you have met...
Your "MY★KU" will now be set!

Positive
Thinking
Should
Develop

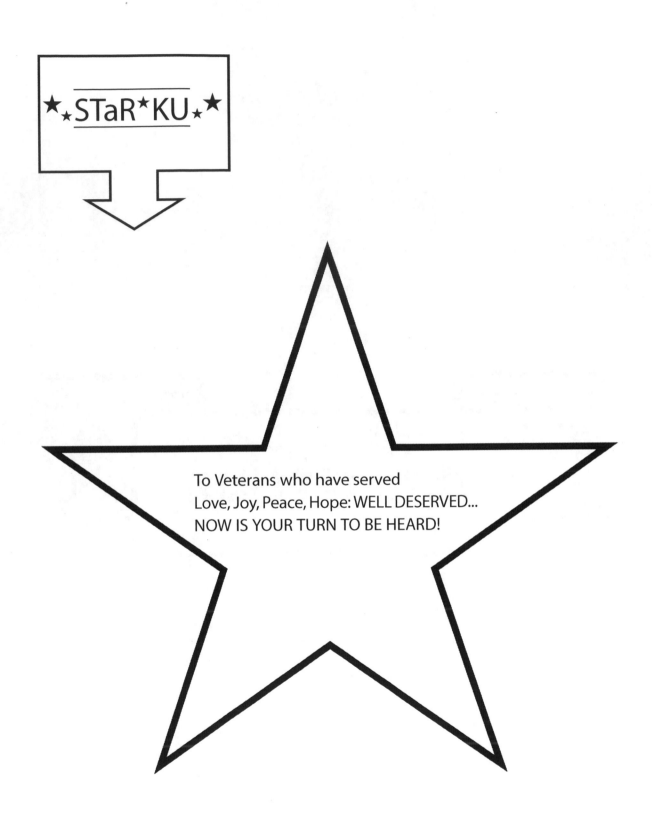

★.STaR★KU.★

To Veterans who have served
Love, Joy, Peace, Hope: WELL DESERVED...
NOW IS YOUR TURN TO BE HEARD!

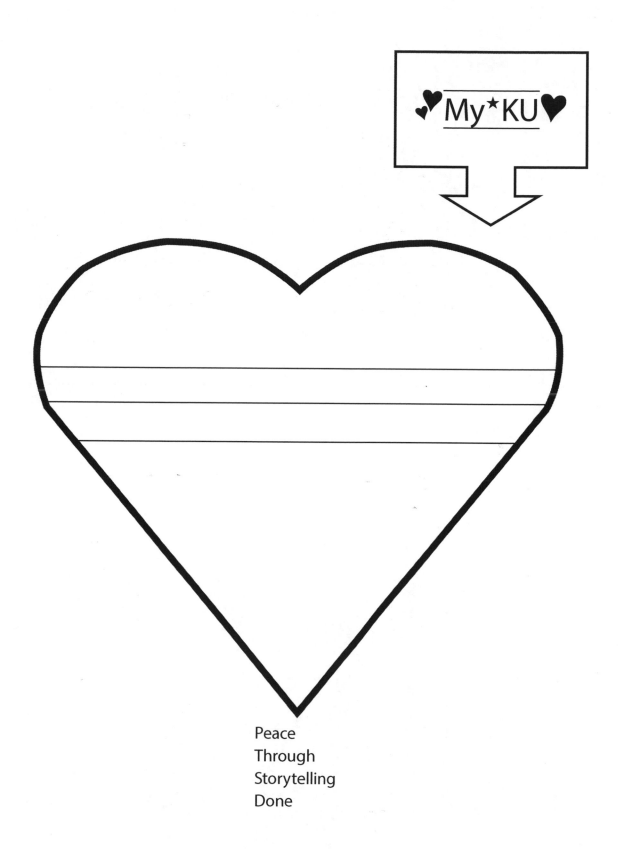

Peace
Through
Storytelling
Done

HAPPINESS

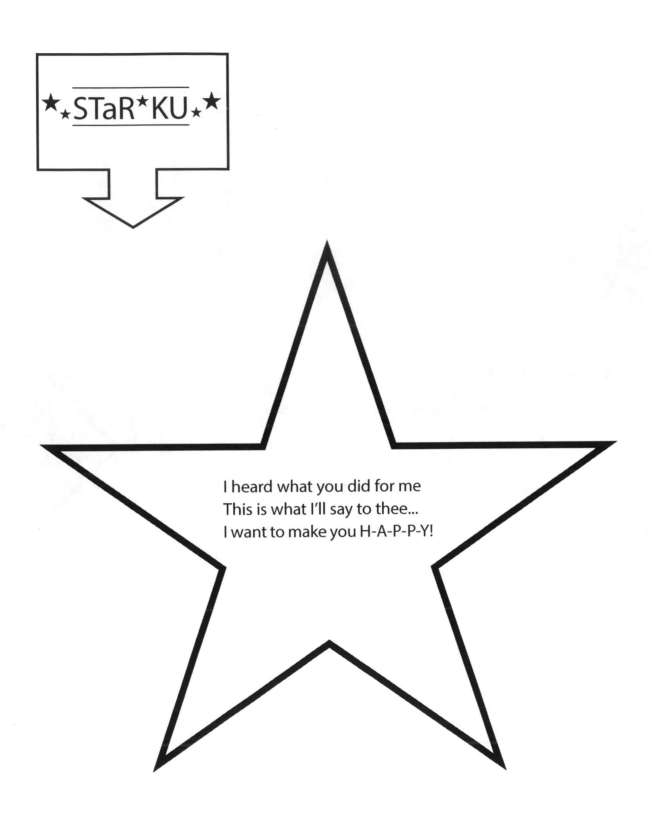

I heard what you did for me
This is what I'll say to thee...
I want to make you H-A-P-P-Y!

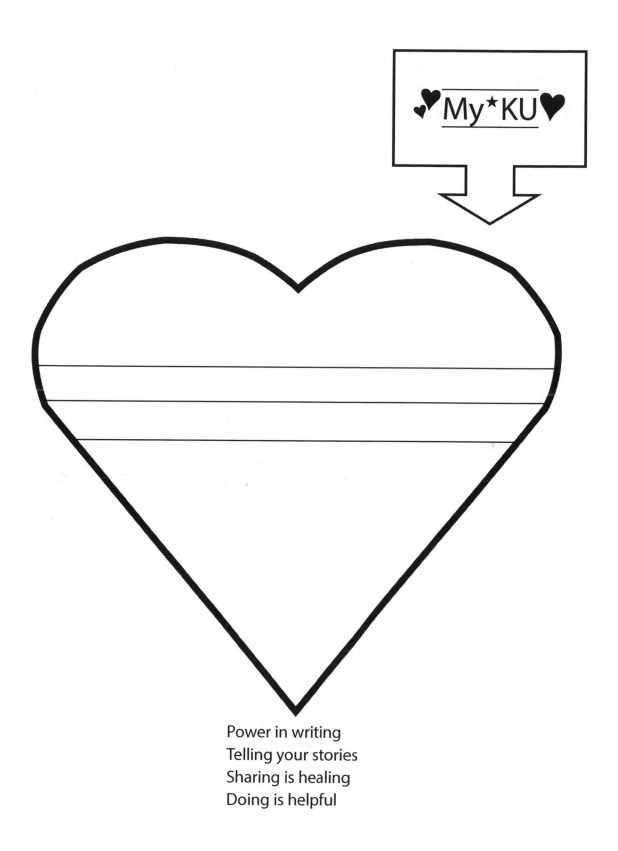

Power in writing
Telling your stories
Sharing is healing
Doing is helpful

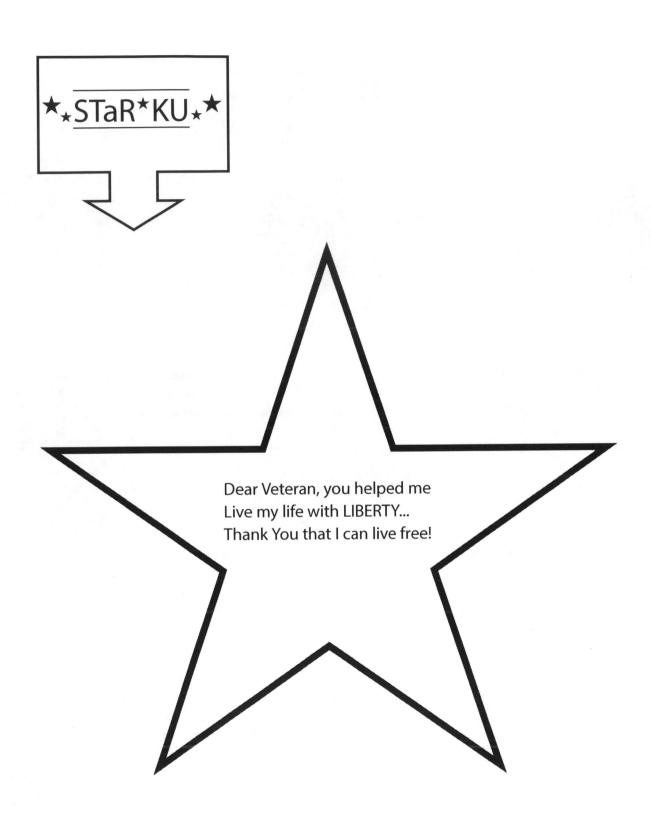

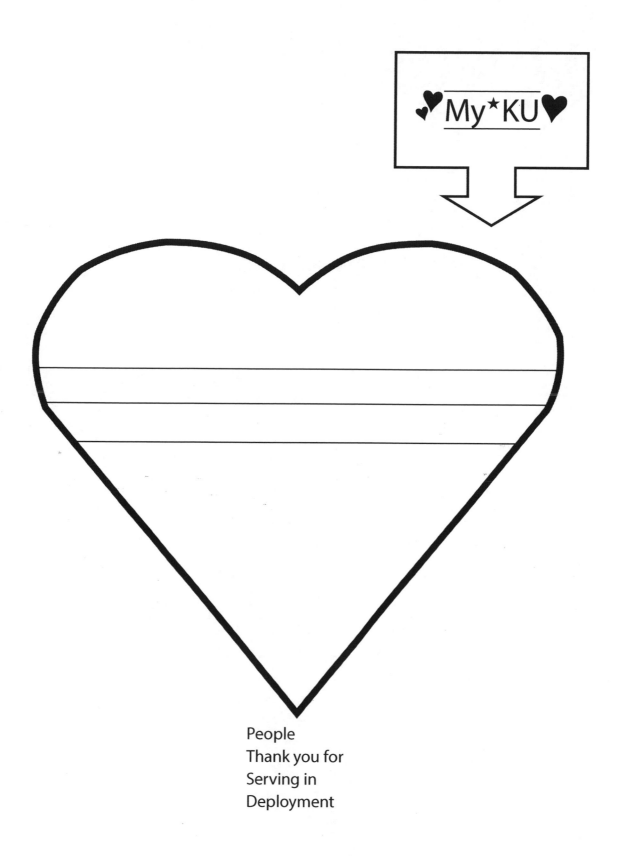

People
Thank you for
Serving in
Deployment

HONOR

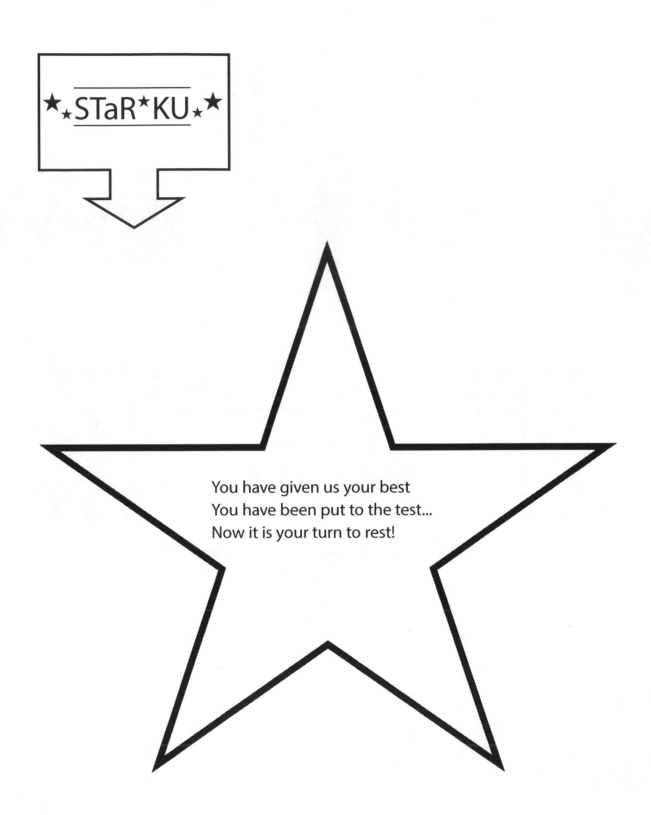

Peace within
Telling my stories...
Success in writing 'My*KU'
Daily

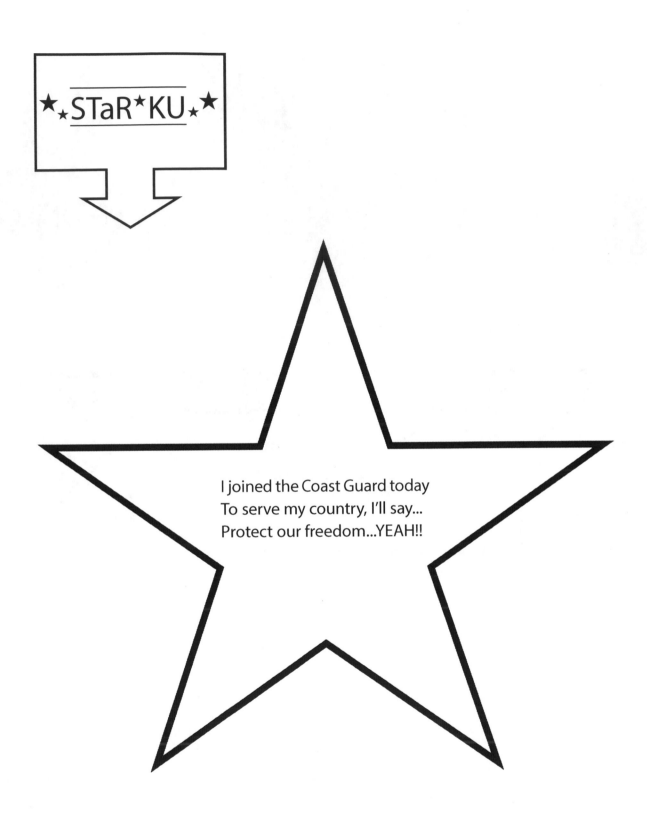

Post
Traumatic
Stress
Disorder

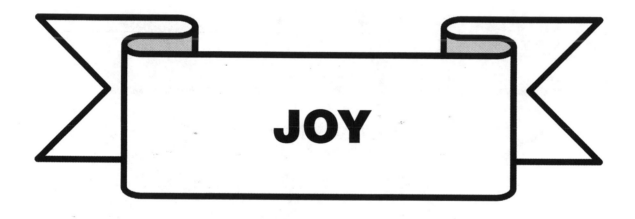

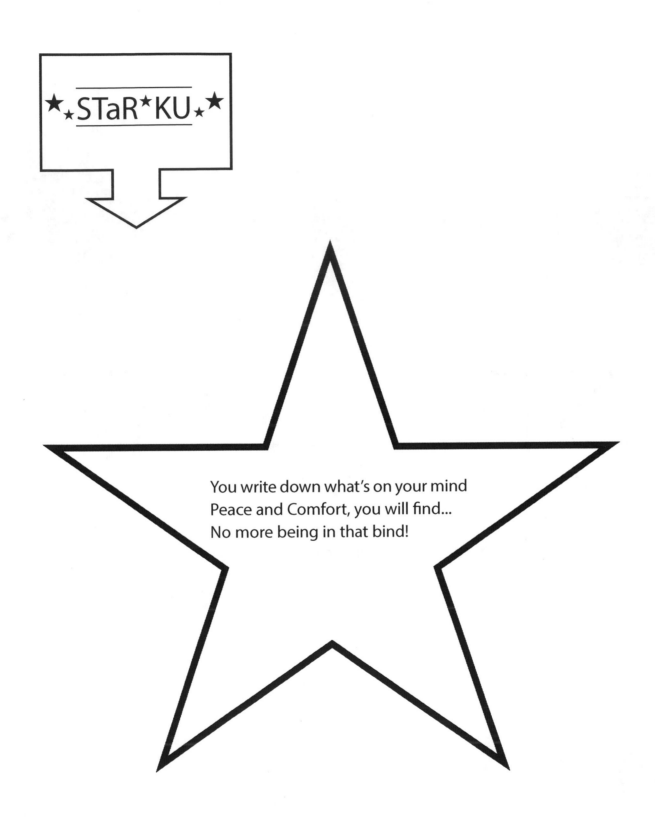

★⋆STaR★KU⋆★

You write down what's on your mind
Peace and Comfort, you will find...
No more being in that bind!

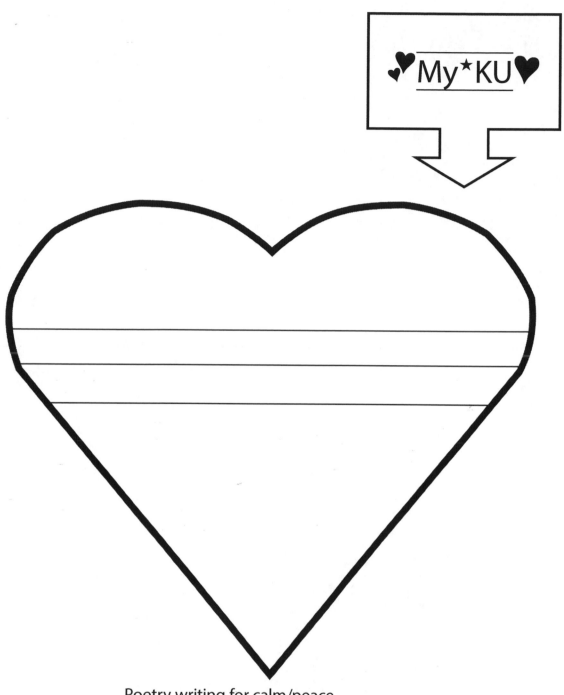

Poetry writing for calm/peace
Telling about events in poetry
Story telling of stressful events in poetry
Documenting stressful events in poetry

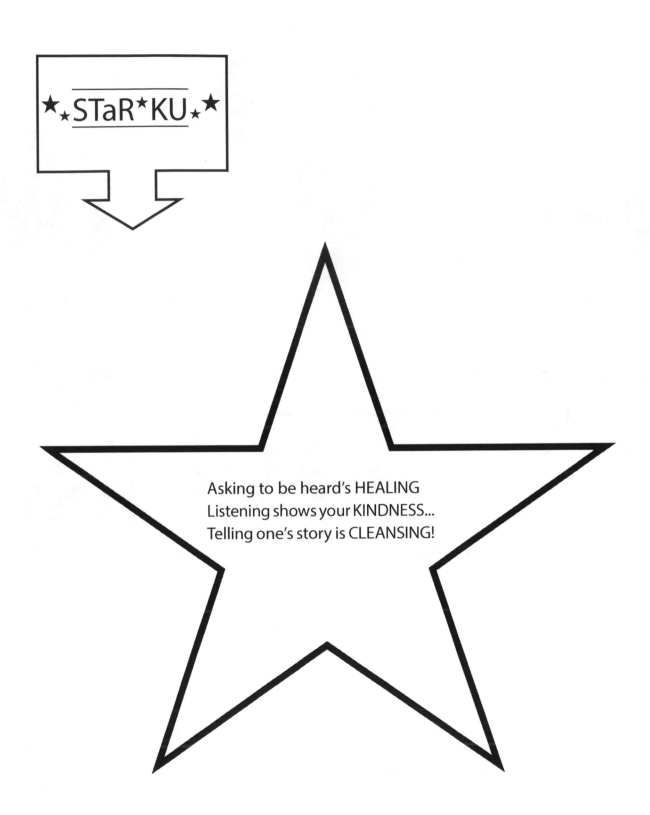

★.STaR★KU.★

Asking to be heard's HEALING
Listening shows your KINDNESS...
Telling one's story is CLEANSING!

Peace
Through
Storytelling/Poetry (MY*KU)
Do it!!!

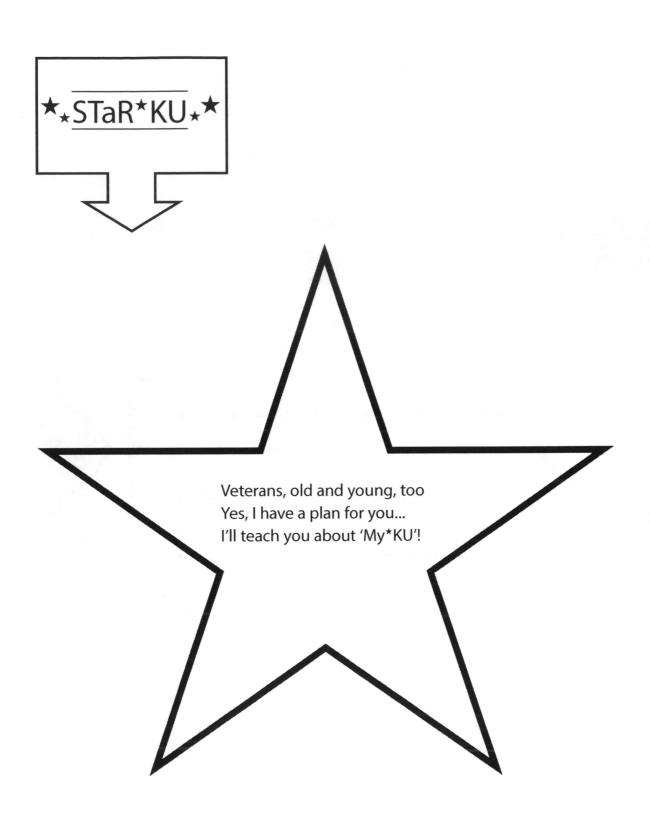

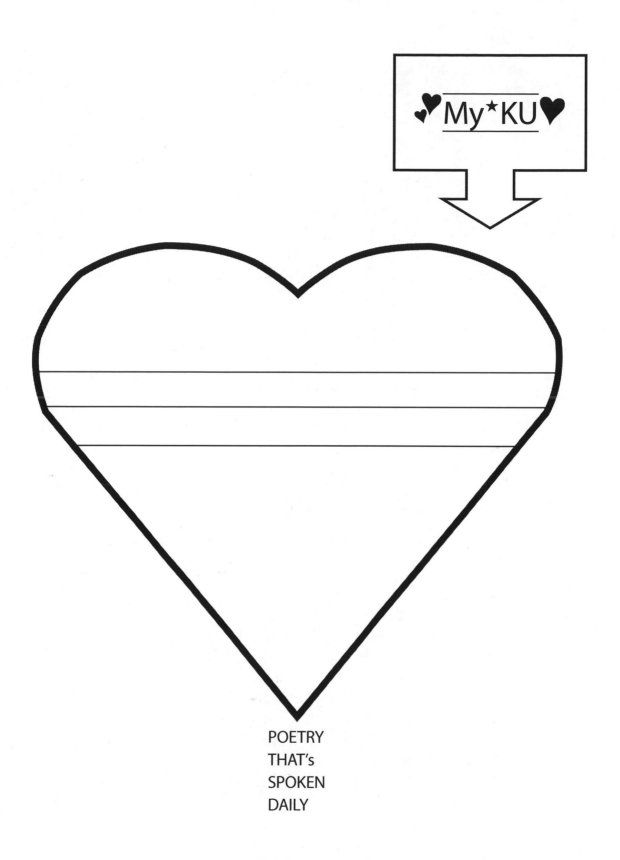

POETRY
THAT's
SPOKEN
DAILY

LEARNING

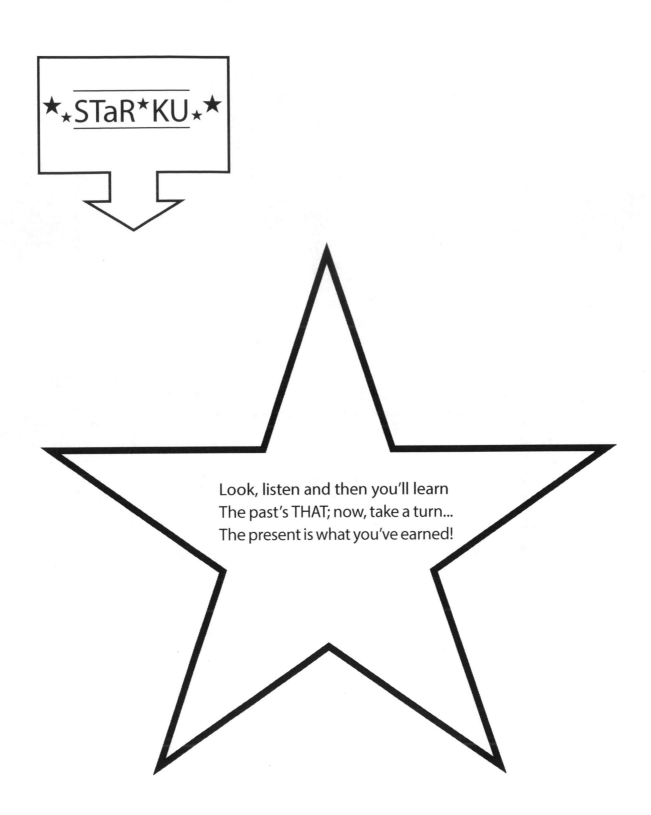

STaR*KU

Look, listen and then you'll learn
The past's THAT; now, take a turn...
The present is what you've earned!

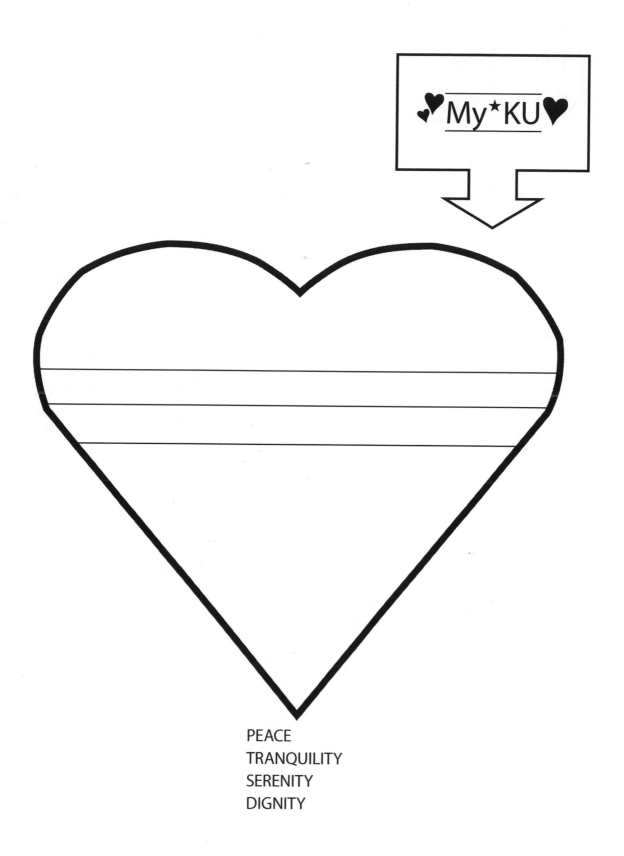

PEACE
TRANQUILITY
SERENITY
DIGNITY

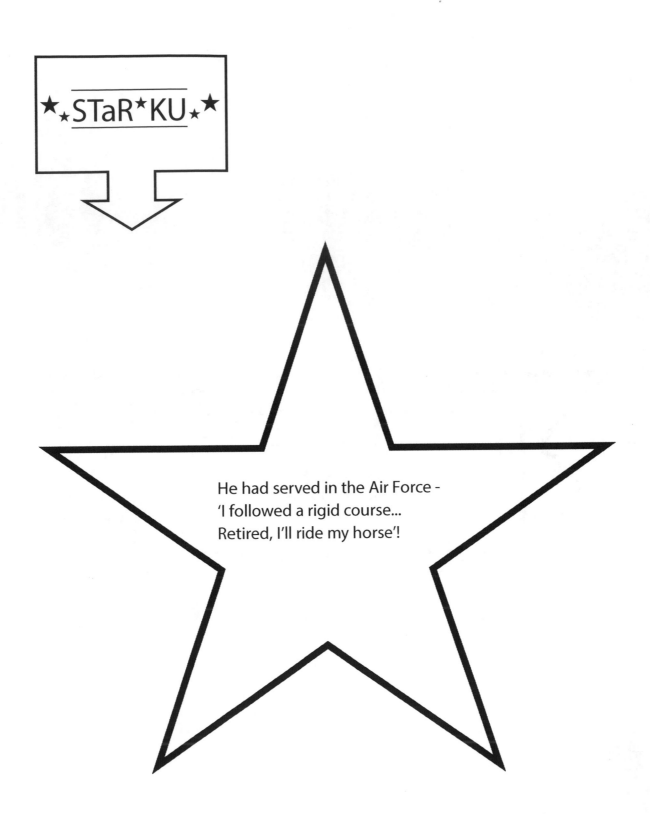

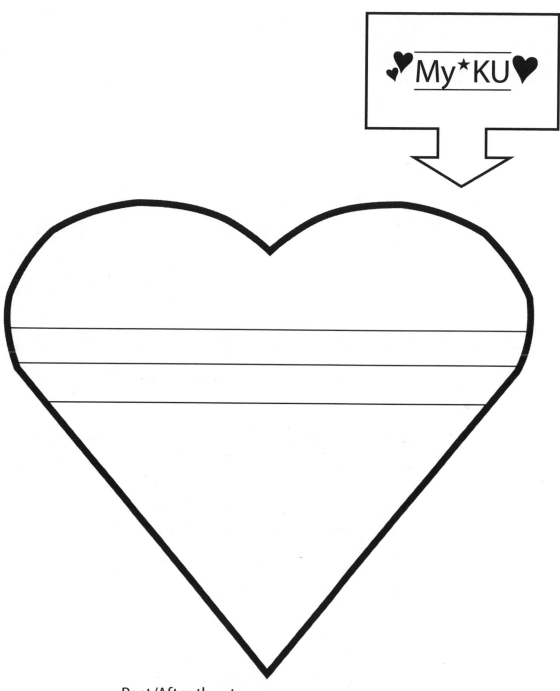

Post/After the storm
Traumatic thoughts
Storytelling of events...
Documenting traumatic events in poetry

LOVE

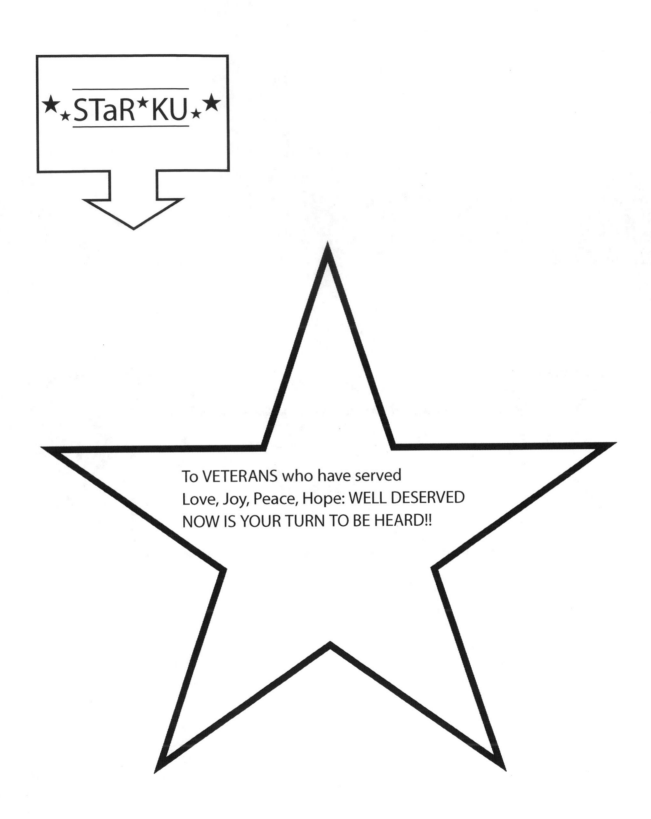

To VETERANS who have served
Love, Joy, Peace, Hope: WELL DESERVED
NOW IS YOUR TURN TO BE HEARD!!

Putting
The
Story
Down

MISSION

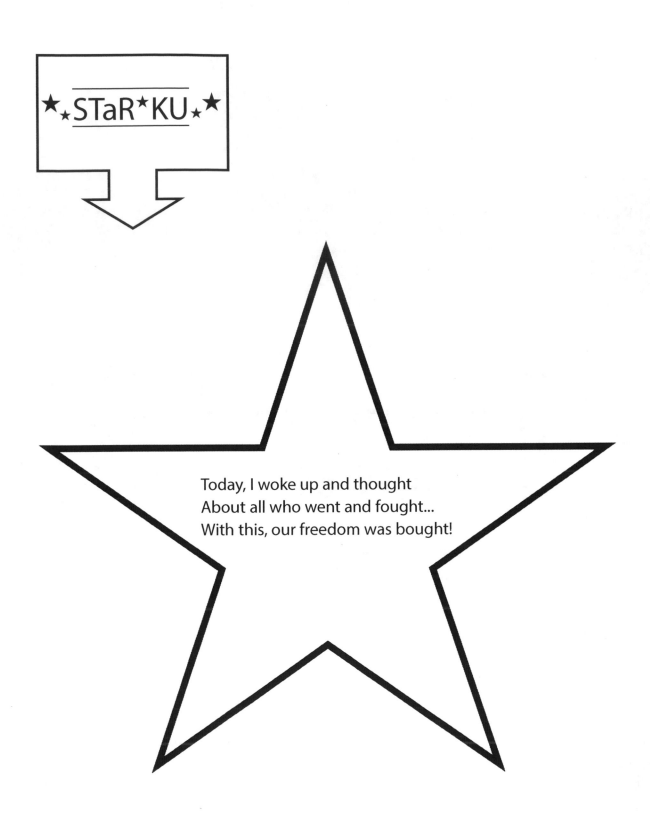

★ ★ STaR★KU ★ ★

Today, I woke up and thought
About all who went and fought...
With this, our freedom was bought!

Peace
Tranquility
Serenity
Divine intervention

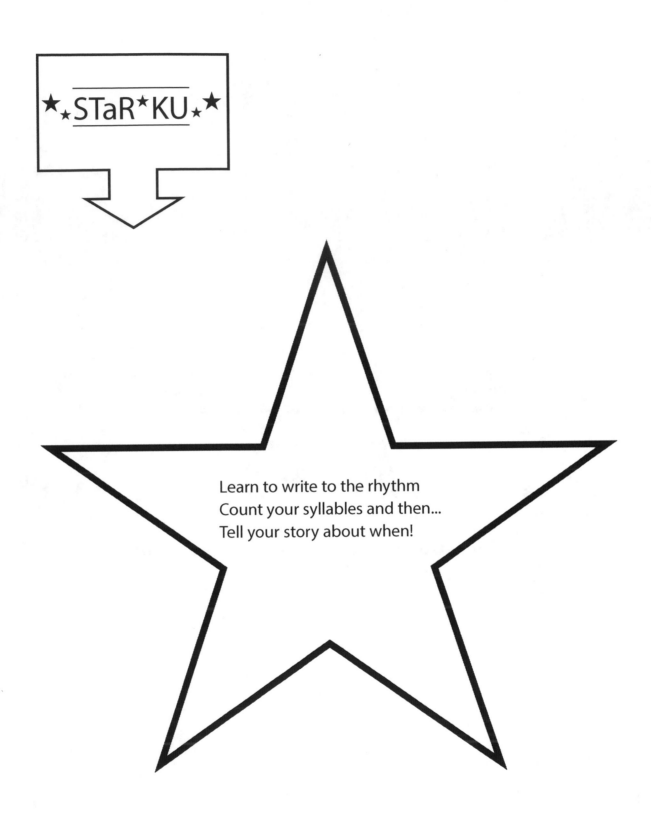

★.STaR★KU.★

Learn to write to the rhythm
Count your syllables and then...
Tell your story about when!

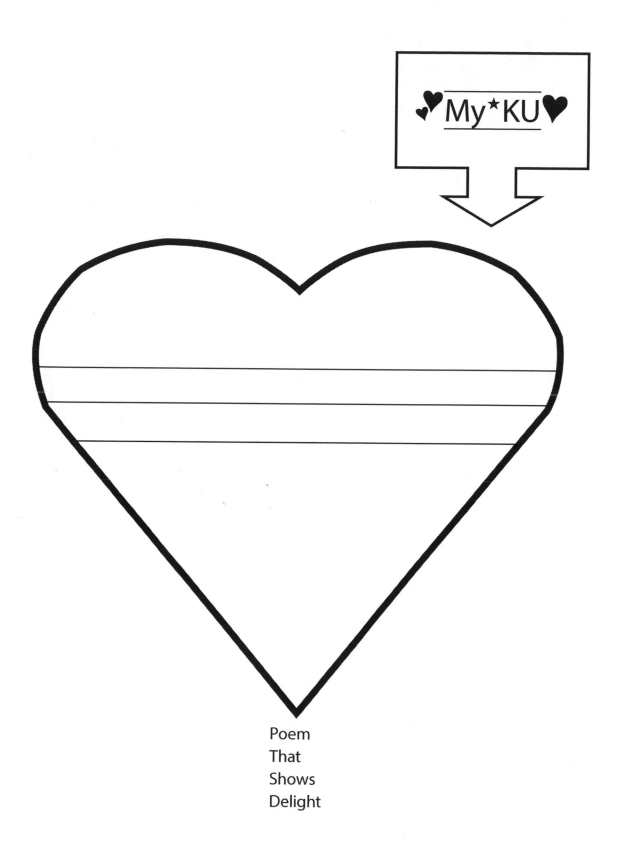

Poem
That
Shows
Delight

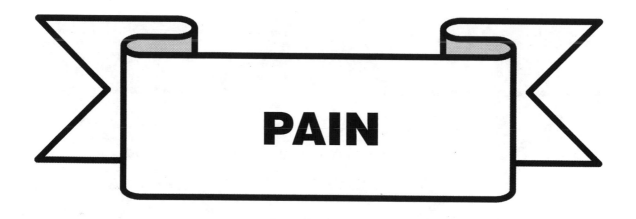

PAIN

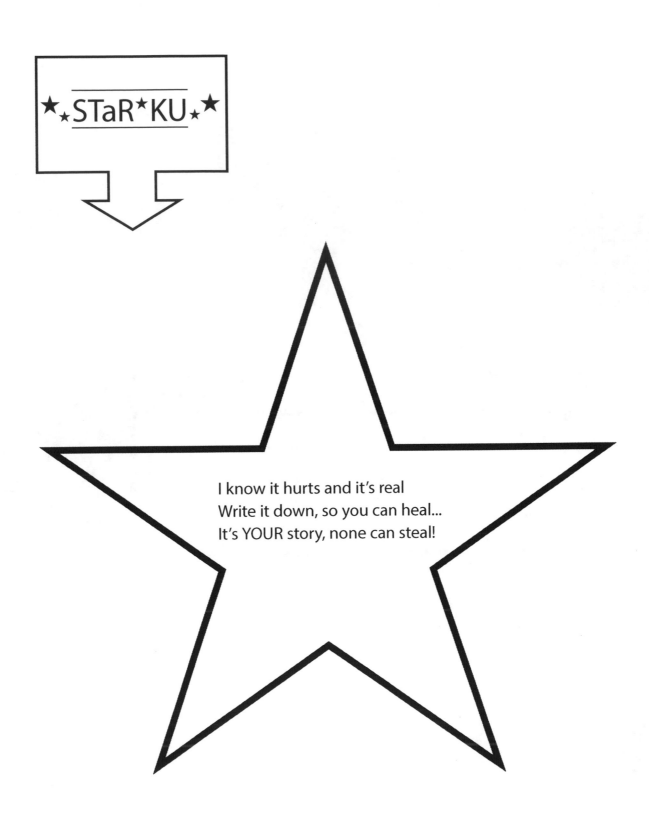

Power in writing
Telling your stories
Sharing is healing
Divine enlightenment

PEACE

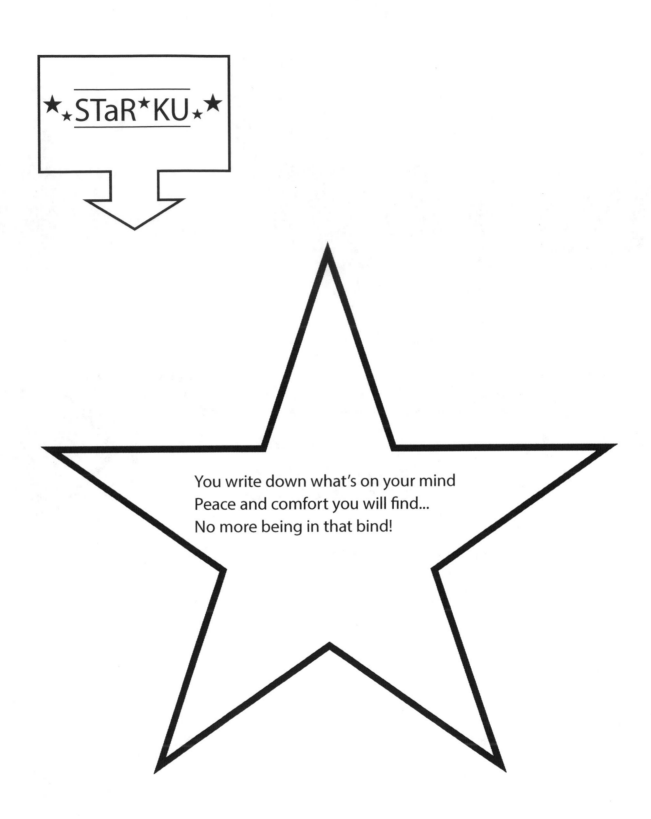

★.STaR★KU.★

You write down what's on your mind
Peace and comfort you will find...
No more being in that bind!

92

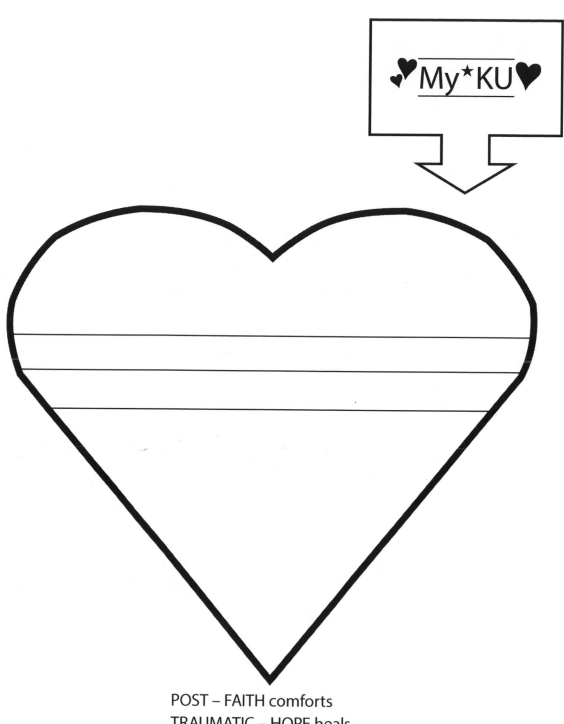

POST – FAITH comforts
TRAUMATIC – HOPE heals
STRESS – LOVE relives
DISORDER – PEACE restores

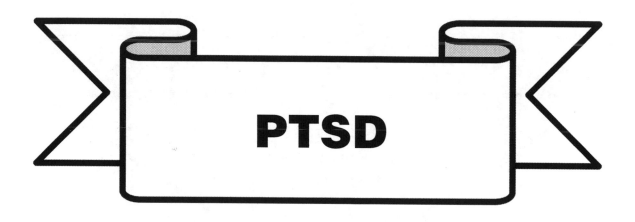

PTSD

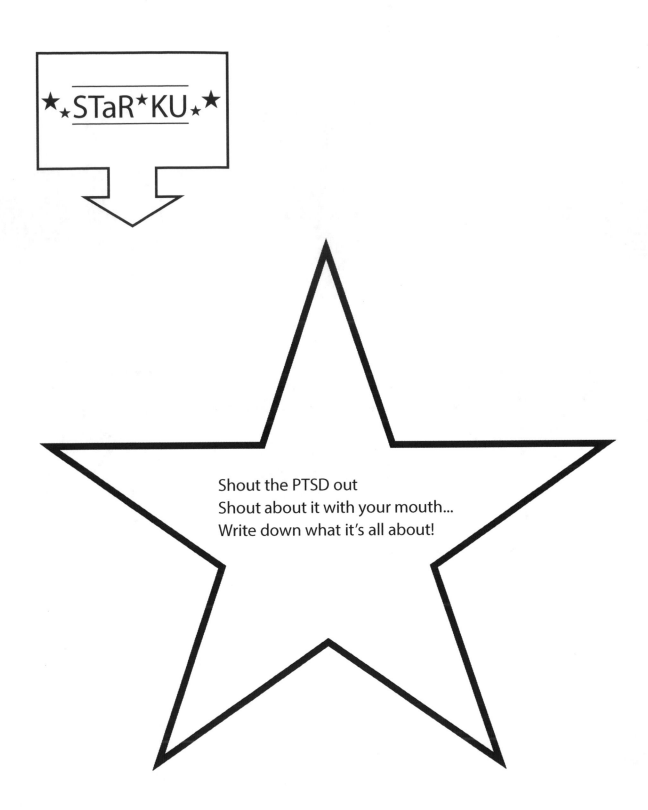

Shout the PTSD out
Shout about it with your mouth...
Write down what it's all about!

Poem
That
Says
Done

PURPOSE

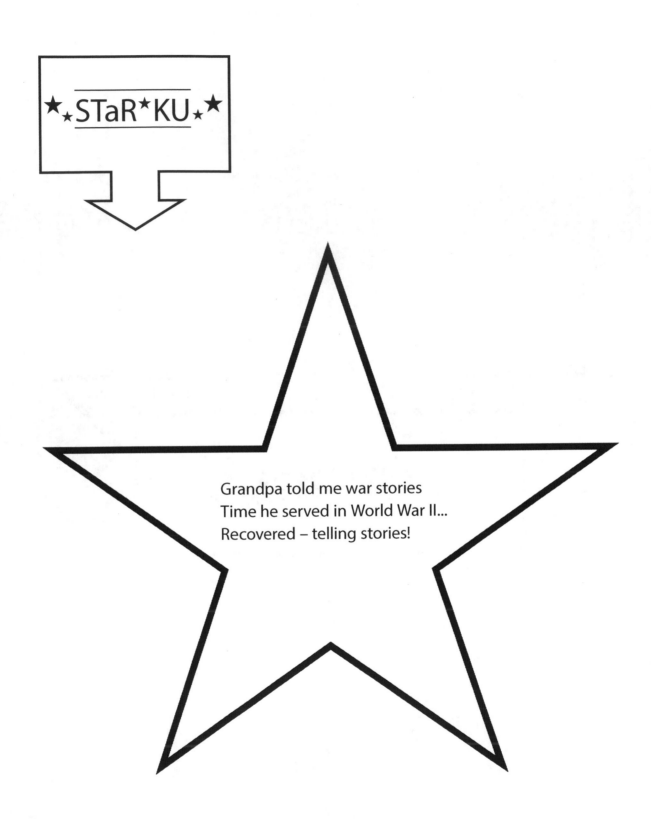

STaR★KU

Grandpa told me war stories
Time he served in World War II...
Recovered – telling stories!

Power in writing
Telling your stories
Sharing is Healing
Divine enlightenment!

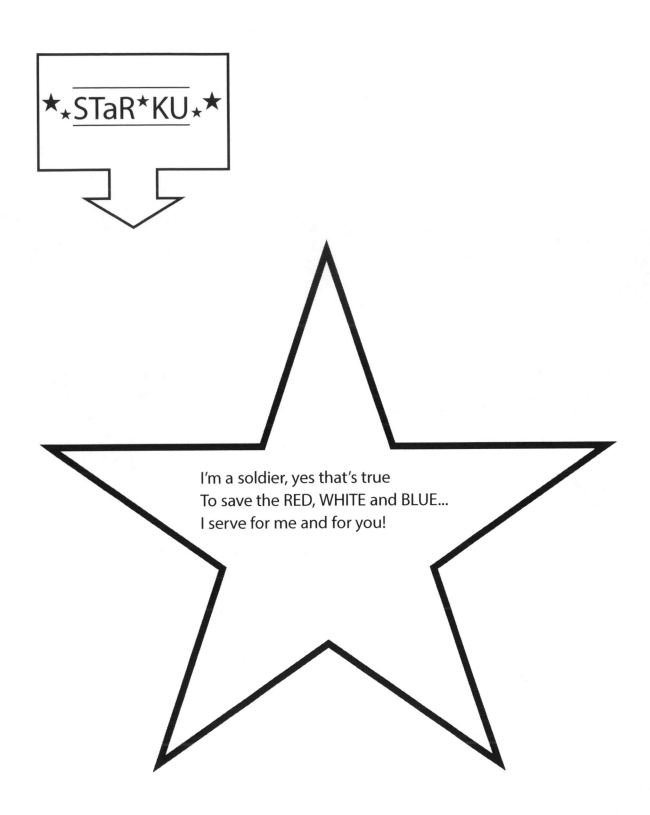

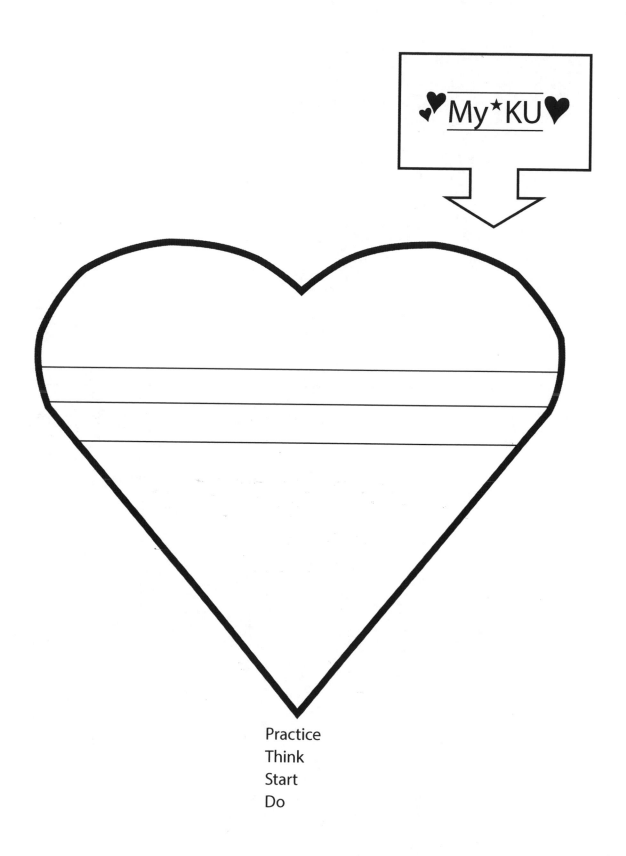

Practice
Think
Start
Do

SERVING

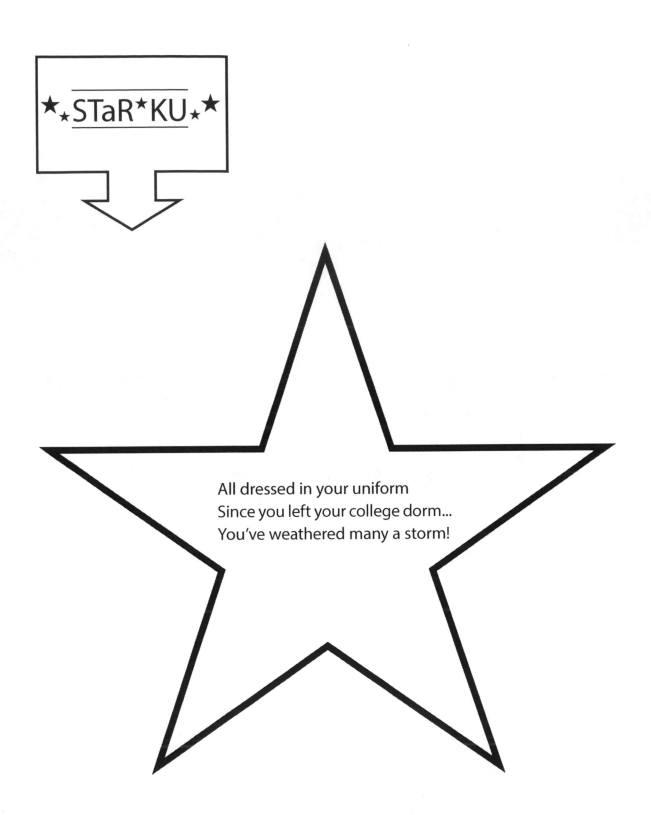

All dressed in your uniform
Since you left your college dorm...
You've weathered many a storm!

PURPOSE
TRUST
SERVICE
DIGNITY

SHARING/ CARING

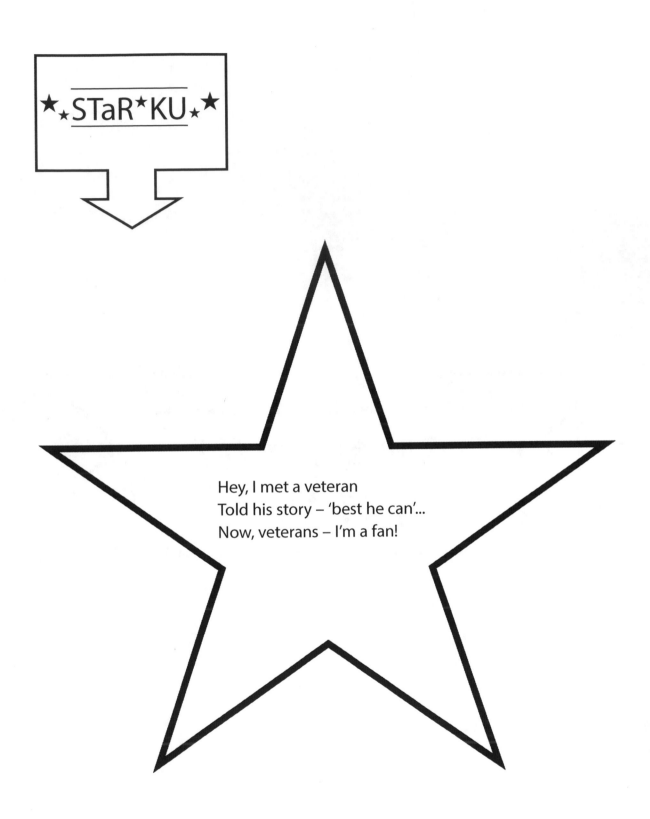

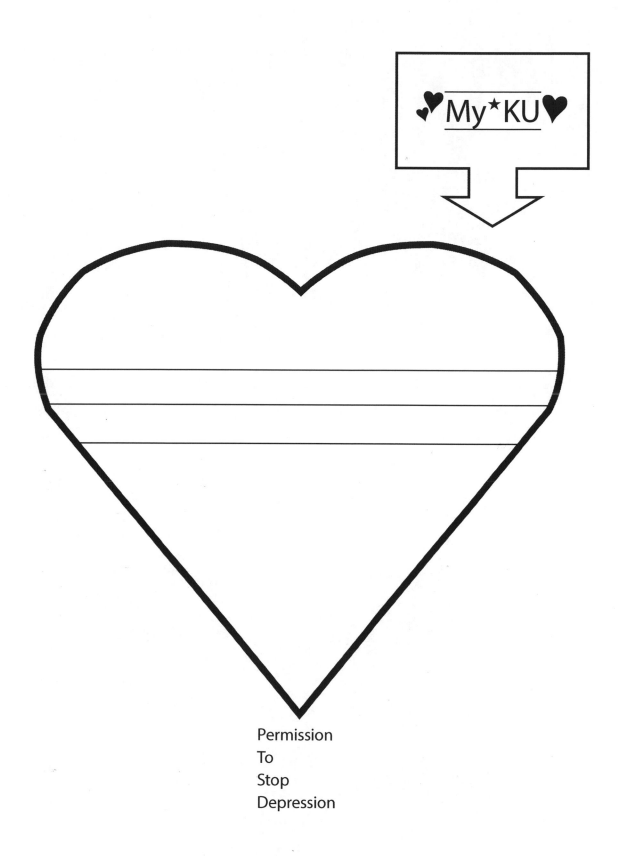

Permission
To
Stop
Depression

STORYTELLING

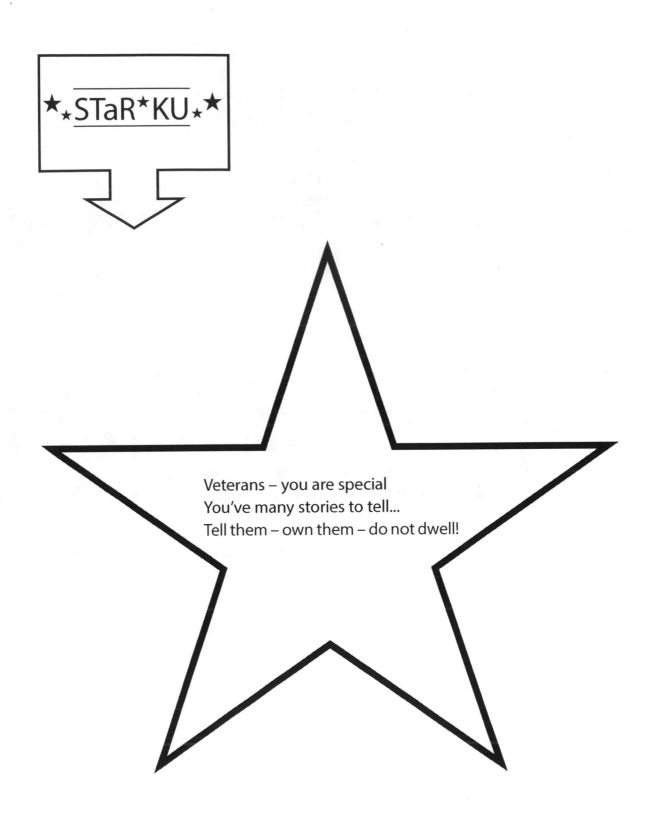

★.‾STaR★KU.★

Veterans – you are special
You've many stories to tell...
Tell them – own them – do not dwell!

Putting
Tragic
Stories
Down, poetically!

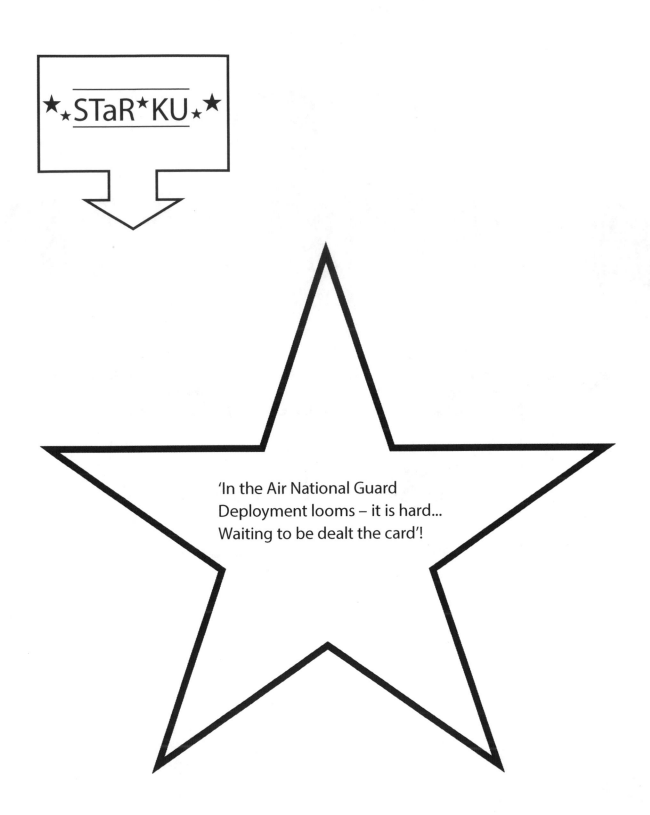

Permission
To
Stop
Depressing memories

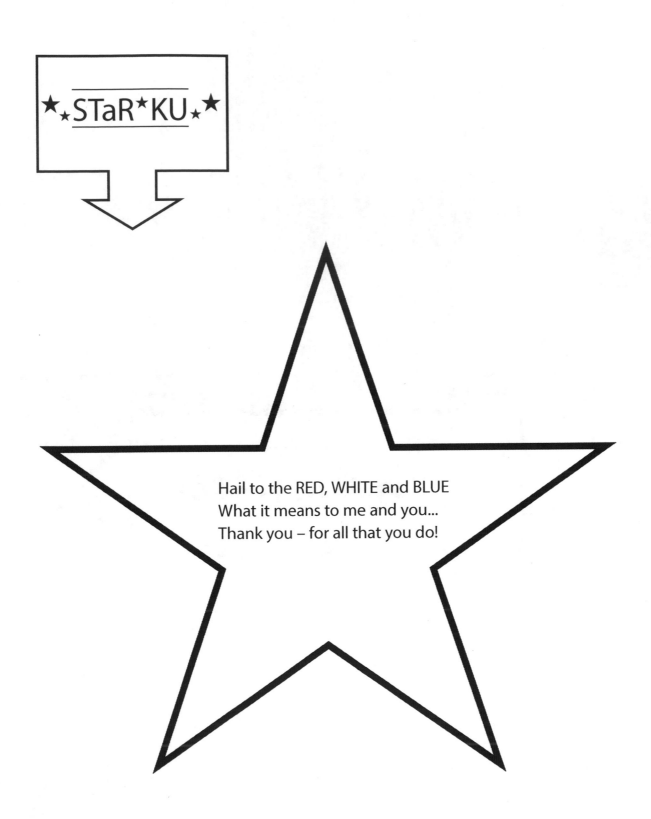

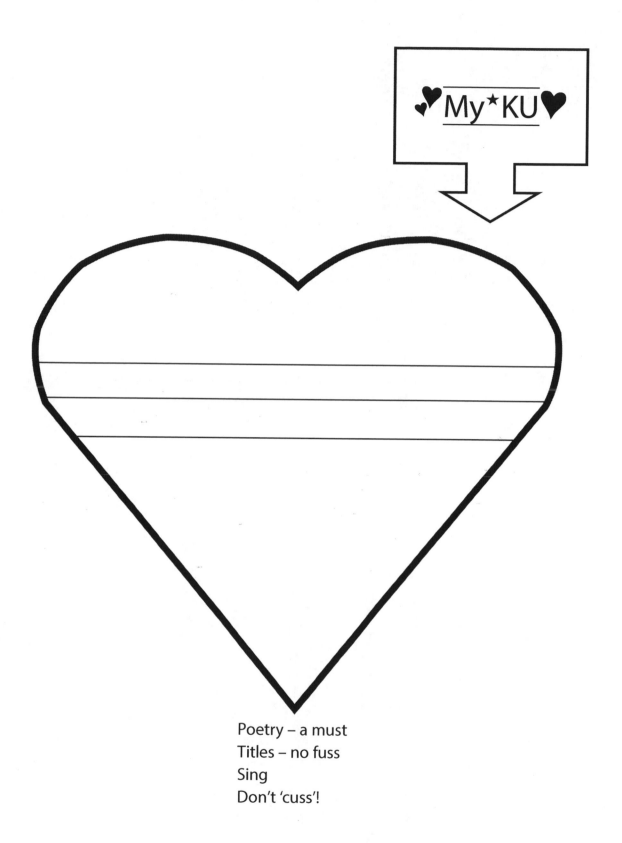

Poetry – a must
Titles – no fuss
Sing
Don't 'cuss'!

TRAUMA

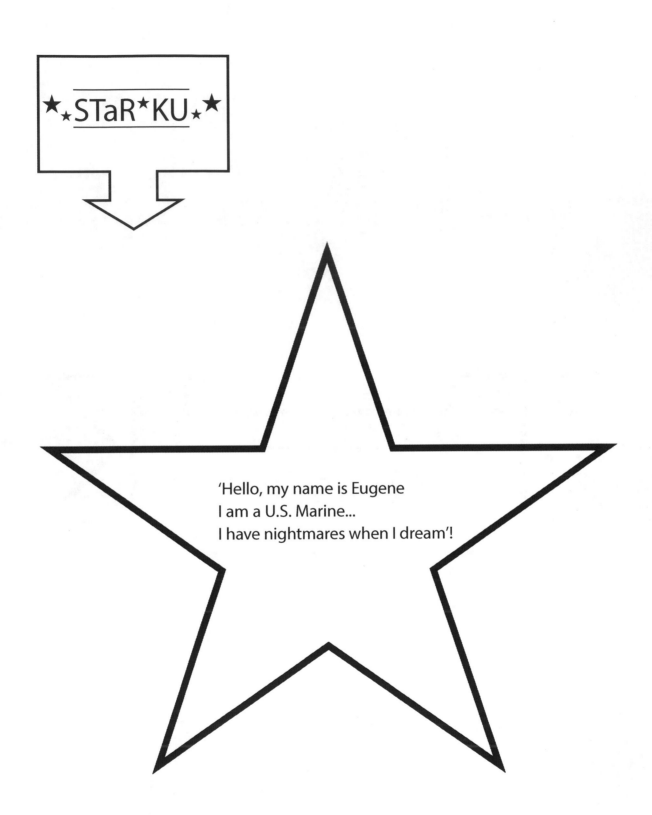

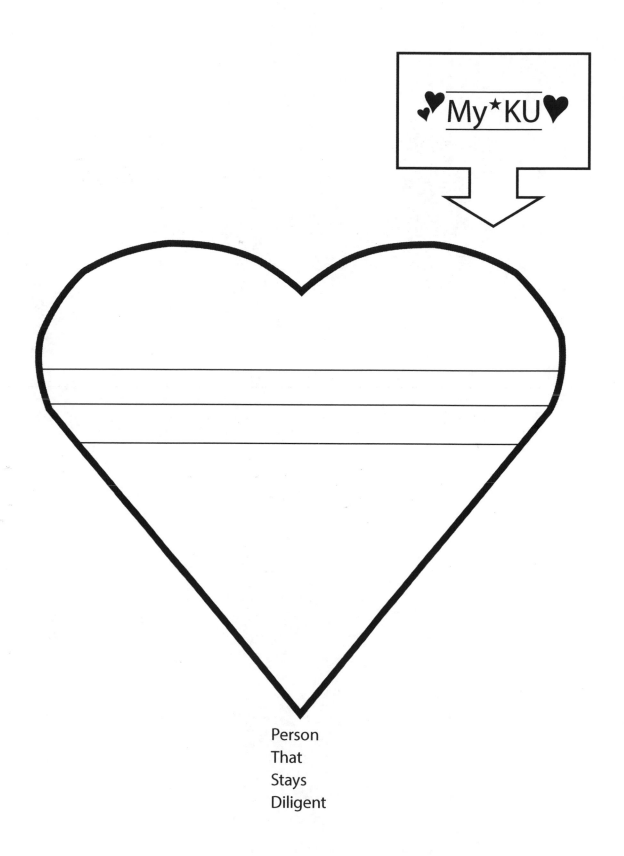

Person
That
Stays
Diligent

TRUST

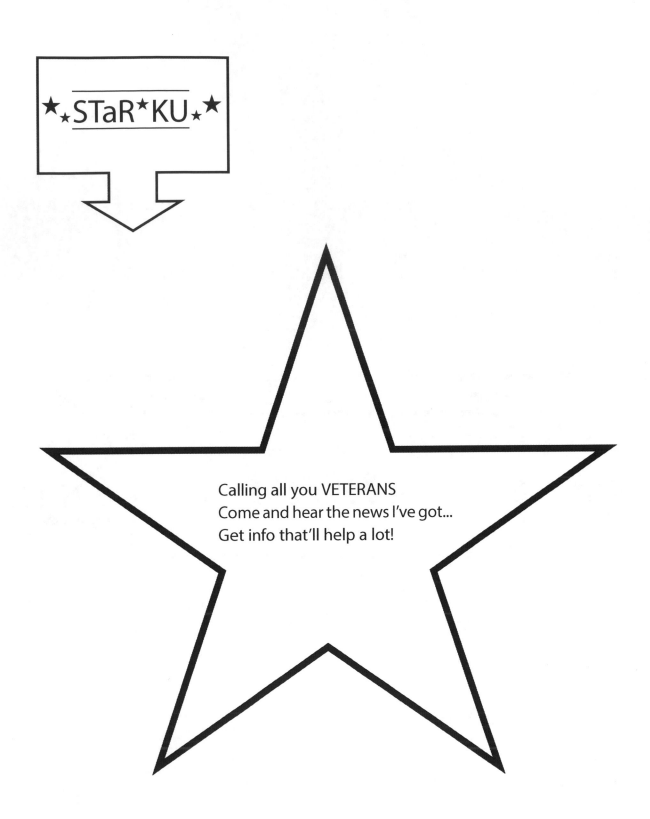

Poetry
That
Seeks
Decision

ULTIMATE SACRIFICE

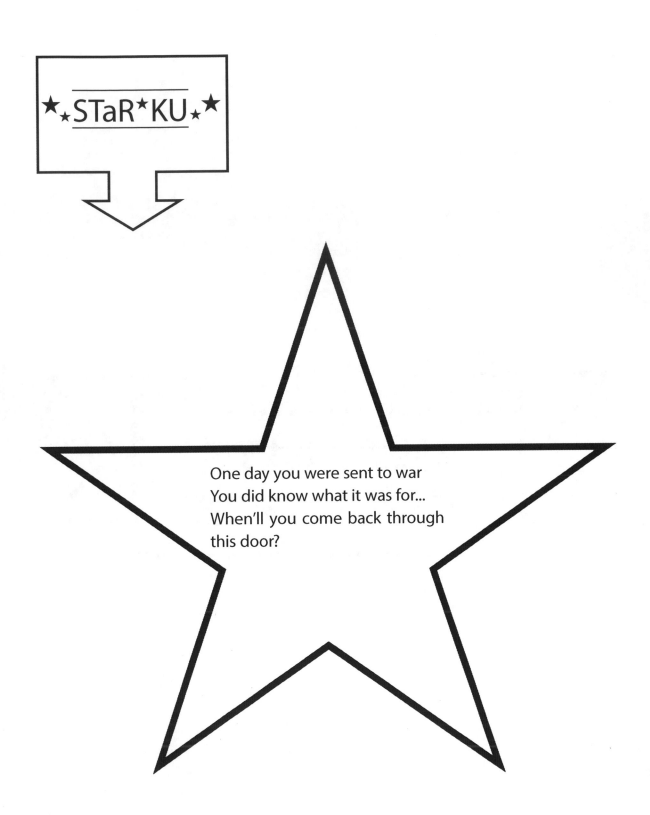

One day you were sent to war
You did know what it was for...
When'll you come back through
this door?

Poetry
Telling
Stories...
DONE!

VETERAN

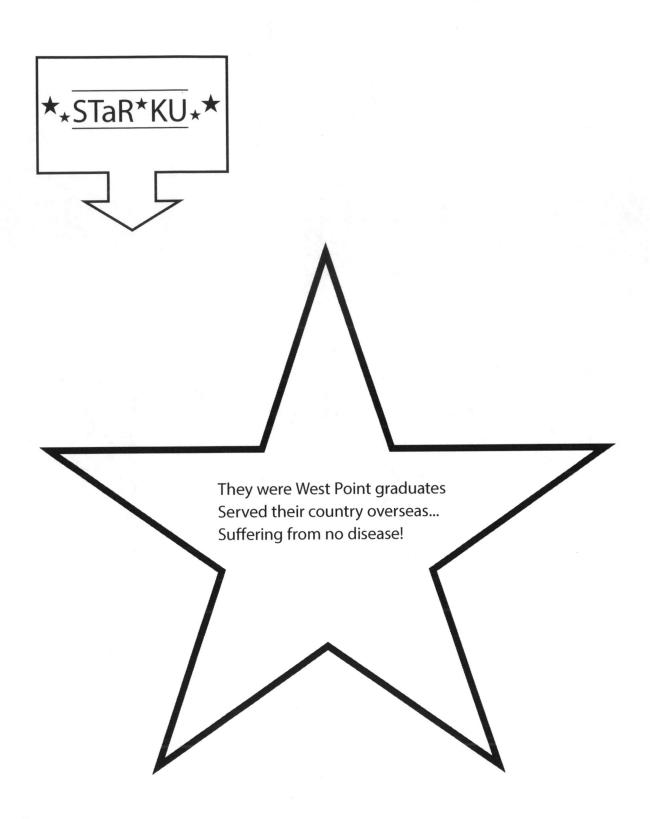

STaR★KU

They were West Point graduates
Served their country overseas...
Suffering from no disease!

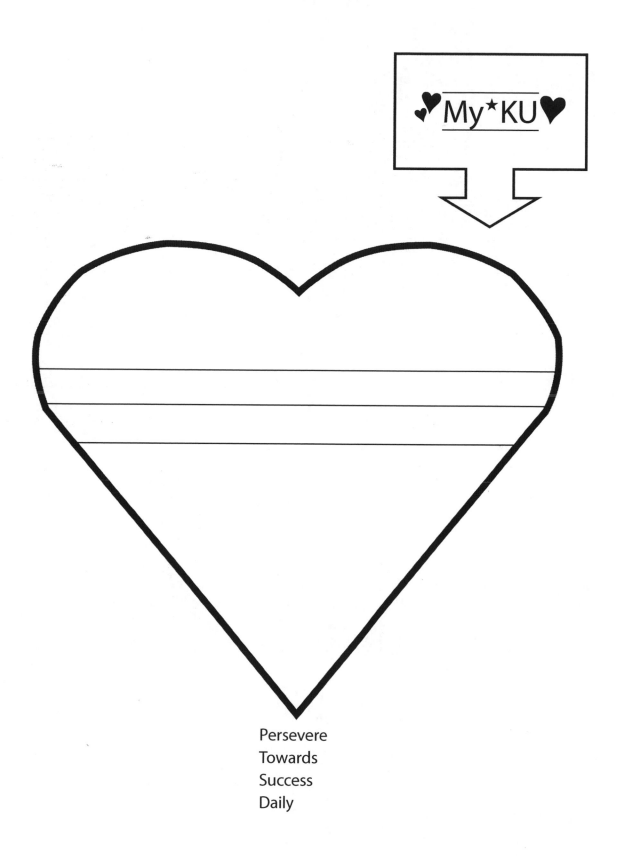

Persevere
Towards
Success
Daily

VULNERABILITY

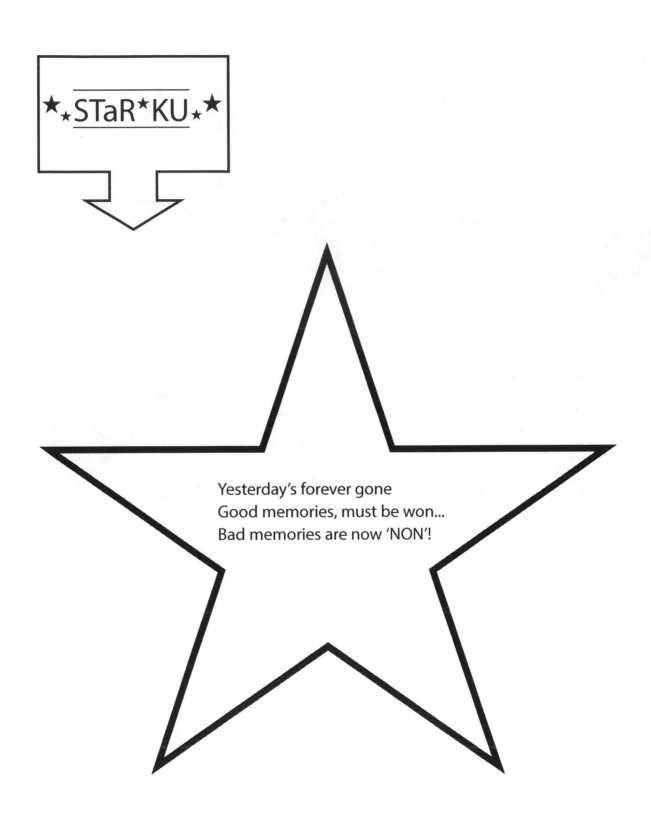

Yesterday's forever gone
Good memories, must be won...
Bad memories are now 'NON'!

Poetry
That
Seeks
Decision

'ISM's to live by

GIVING<--------------->GETTING

ASKING to be heard is HEALING
TELLING one's story is CLEANSING
LISTENING to what needs to be said is KINDNESS

HELPING YOU<--------------------------->HELPING OTHERS...
HELPING YOU<~~~~~~~~~~~~~~~~~~~~~~>YOU HELPED ME

                                                         THANK YOU!!!

Post<===========>Peace
Traumatic<===========>Through====>POETRY (MY*KU)
Stress<===========>Storytelling
Disorder<=======>DONE!

Peace within through
Telling my stories...
Success in writing 'My*KU'
Daily

MY*KU
MANTRA

Poetry
Trust
Self Awareness
Documented

STaRism's

- **Opportunity + Perseverance = Success**
- **Time, Energy and Money = Living**
- **Appreciation + Gratitude = Hope**
- **Gratitude + Aptitude = Attitude**
- **Comfort + Joy = Love**
- **Love + Hope = Peace**
- **Peace + Comfort = Happiness**
- **Prayer + Faith = Blessings**
- **Working + Caring = Satisfaction**
- **Striving + Fulfilling = Joy**
- **Past + Present = Future**
- **Thought + Touch = Change**
- **Information + Investigation = Imagination**
- **Resistance + Assistance = Sustenance**
- **Search + Faith = Discovery**
- **Dream it + Believe it = Become it**
- **Confidence + Intensity = 'Winning'**
- **Observation + Opinion = Decision**
- **Intelligence + Personality = a Gift**
- **Inspiration + Motivation = Confidence**
- **Compassion + Empathy = Caring**
- **Proactivity + positivity = Opportunity**
- **Humility + Confidence = Ability**
- **Hope + Joy + Love + Peace = Sacred Treasures**

OPPORTUNITY + PERSEVERANCE = SUCCESS

Should you have any questions please feel free to
email me at: myku789@gmail.com

Printed in the United States
By Bookmasters